contents

NZ, Canada, US and UK readers
Please note that Australian cup and
spoon measurements are metric.
A conversion chart appears on page 62.

casseroles

Nothing is more mouth-watering than the aroma of a homely casserole or tangy curry simmering on the stove: these one-pot wonders offer warmth and comfort, and they have something else going for them too: in the main, they usually cost less to make than a classic meat, salad and vegie dinner.

One-pot meals generally use less expensive cuts of meat, such as gravy beef, shanks, neck or shoulder. These more sinewy cuts need slow cooking to bring out their great depth of flavour and melt-in-the-mouth tenderness. Don't discount casseroles and curries when you entertain either: served with steamed rice or fresh bread, they make an impressive meal. They'll also help keep your stress levels down since they can be made ahead, and are as good or better when reheated on the second day.

Traditionally, curry paste is made with a mortar and pestle but, for ease and speed, we made ours in a blender or food processor. Any remaining paste can be sealed and refrigerated or frozen after you've used what you need in a recipe. It can be kept this way for up to three months with no discernible difference in flavour.

There are many curry pastes available at Asian grocers and supermarkets, some imported from India and Thailand and others made locally. If you don't want to make your own, these will do the job more than adequately. This guide will help you tell them apart:

balti Taking its name from Baltistan, a region in northern Pakistan, balti is an aromatic, medium-hot paste made with coriander, fenugreek and mint; these fresh green herbs give it a distinctive mild "green" flavour.

& curries

green Hottest of the traditional Thai pastes, it's particularly good in chicken and vegetable curries, and a great addition to stir-fry or noodle dishes.

korma A classic Indian paste typical of the affluent Mogul Empire with its rich, luscious content of almonds, saffron, cream and cardamom.

massaman With spicy flavours hinting of Middle Eastern cooking, this curry was brought to southern Thailand by Muslim traders and is now used in hot and sour stew-like curries and satays.

panang Based on the curries of Penang, an island off the Malaysian coast near the Thai border. A milder variation of red curry paste, it is good with seafood and for adding to soups.

red Probably the most popular Thai curry paste, this is a fiery blend of different flavours that suits the richness of pork, duck and seafood.

rogan josh From Kashmir in India, this medium-hot, deep-red paste is made from fresh chillies or paprika, tomato and aromatic spices.

tikka In Indian cooking, this loosely translates as a non-specific paste for bite-sized pieces of meat, poultry or fish; it can be any maker's choice of spices and oils, and is frequently coloured red. It's used in marinating or for brushing over cooking food, rather than as an ingredient.

vindaloo A Goan paste made of vinegar, tomatoes, pepper and other spices that illustrate the Portuguese influence on India's west coast.

yellow One of the mildest Thai pastes, it's similar in appearance to some Indian pastes because of the inclusion of strongly coloured fresh turmeric. Good mixed with coconut in rice and noodle dishes.

seafood stew with chermoulla

500g black mussels
800g uncooked medium
  king prawns
300g kingfish fillet,
  skin removed
1 squid hood (150g)
1 tablespoon olive oil
1 large brown onion (200g),
  chopped finely
3 cloves garlic, crushed
1 medium red capsicum
  (200g), chopped finely
½ cup (125ml) dry white wine
1 cup (250ml) fish stock
425g can diced tomatoes
chermoulla
½ cup finely chopped
  fresh coriander
½ cup finely chopped
  fresh flat-leaf parsley
1 clove garlic, crushed
2 tablespoons white
  wine vinegar
2 tablespoons lemon juice
½ teaspoon ground cumin
2 tablespoons olive oil

1 Scrub mussels; remove beards. Shell and devein prawns, leaving tails intact. Cut fish into 3cm pieces. Cut squid down centre to open out; score inside in diagonal pattern then cut into thick strips.

2 Heat oil in large saucepan; cook onion, garlic and capsicum, stirring, until onion softens. Stir in wine; cook, uncovered, until wine is almost evaporated. Add stock and undrained tomatoes; bring to a boil. Add seafood, reduce heat; simmer, covered, about 5 minutes or until squid is tender and mussels open (discard any that do not).

3 Stir half the chermoulla into stew. Divide stew among bowls; sprinkle with remaining chermoulla. Serve with a warmed baguette, if desired.

chermoulla Combine ingredients in small bowl.

serves 4
preparation time 30 minutes
cooking time 30 minutes
per serving 17.5g total fat (3g saturated fat); 1714kJ (410 cal); 8.7g carbohydrate; 48.6g protein; 3.5g fibre
tips Keep freshly made chermoulla in the refrigerator, covered with a thin layer of olive oil, for up to a month.
This recipe is not suitable to make in a slow cooker or pressure cooker.

octopus in red wine

1 tablespoon olive oil
2kg whole cleaned baby octopus, quartered
2 cloves garlic, crushed
20 baby brown onions (500g), quartered
2 bay leaves
1½ cups (375ml) dry red wine
1 cup (250ml) chicken stock
¼ cup (60ml) red wine vinegar
400g can tomato puree
2 teaspoons dried oregano
2 teaspoons white sugar
1 tablespoon coarsely chopped fresh flat-leaf parsley

1 Heat oil in large saucepan; cook octopus and garlic, stirring, until almost dry.
2 Add onion, bay leaves, wine, stock, vinegar and puree. Bring to a boil; reduce heat, simmer, uncovered, about 1½ hours or until octopus is tender.
3 Remove bay leaves then add oregano and sugar. Serve sprinkled with parsley.

serves 4
preparation time 25 minutes
cooking time 1 hour 45 minutes
per serving 9.9g total fat (1.9g saturated fat); 2178kJ (521 cal); 18.2g carbohydrate; 72.9g protein; 4.2g fibre
tip This recipe is suitable to make in a slow cooker and pressure cooker.

chicken stuffed with ricotta, basil and prosciutto

8 chicken thigh cutlets (1.6kg)
⅔ cup (130g) ricotta cheese
4 slices prosciutto (60g),
   halved lengthways
8 large fresh basil leaves
1 tablespoon olive oil
1 medium brown onion (150g),
   chopped finely
1 medium carrot (120g),
   chopped finely
1 trimmed celery stalk (100g),
   chopped finely
2 cloves garlic, chopped finely
2 tablespoons tomato paste
½ cup (125ml) dry white wine
8 small tomatoes (720g),
   peeled, chopped coarsely
425g can diced tomatoes
½ cup (125ml) water

1 Preheat oven to 160°C/140°C fan-forced.
2 Using small sharp knife, cut a pocket through the thickest part of each cutlet over the bone; push 1 tablespoon of the cheese, one slice of prosciutto and one basil leaf into each pocket. Close pocket; secure with toothpick.
3 Heat oil in large deep flameproof baking dish; cook chicken, in batches, until browned all over.
4 Cook onion, carrot, celery and garlic in same dish, stirring, about 5 minutes or until onion softens. Add paste; cook, stirring, 2 minutes. Add wine; bring to a boil. Reduce heat; simmer, uncovered, 1 minute. Add chopped tomato, undrained canned tomatoes and the water; bring to a boil. Reduce heat; simmer, uncovered, 10 minutes.
5 Return chicken to dish, cover; cook in oven 1 hour. Uncover; cook further 20 minutes or until chicken is cooked through. Remove toothpicks before serving.

serves 4
preparation time 30 minutes
cooking time 2 hours
per serving 46.8g total fat
(15.5g saturated fat); 2922kJ (699 cal);
11.2g carbohydrate; 53.3g protein; 5.5g fibre
tip This recipe is suitable to make in a slow cooker and pressure cooker.

spanish chicken casserole

1 tablespoon olive oil
4 chicken drumsticks (600g)
4 chicken thigh cutlets (800g)
1 large brown onion (200g), chopped finely
4 medium potatoes (800g), quartered
½ cup (80g) roasted pine nuts
½ cup (80g) roasted blanched almonds
3 cups (750ml) chicken stock
1 cup (250ml) dry white wine
⅓ cup (80ml) lemon juice
4 cloves garlic, crushed
2 tablespoons fresh thyme leaves
½ cup coarsely chopped fresh flat-leaf parsley
500g baby green beans, trimmed

1 Preheat oven to 180°C/160°C fan-forced.
2 Heat oil in large flameproof casserole dish; cook chicken, in batches, until browned.
3 Cook onion in same dish, stirring, until soft. Return chicken to dish with potato, nuts, stock, wine, juice, garlic, thyme and half the parsley; bring to a boil. Cover; cook in oven about 1 hour or until chicken is cooked through.
4 Meanwhile, boil, steam or microwave beans until tender; drain.
5 Serve chicken with beans; sprinkle with remaining parsley.

serves 4
preparation time 10 minutes
cooking time 1 hour 25 minutes
per serving 61.4g total fat (12.4g saturated fat); 4050kJ (969 cal); 35g carbohydrate; 57g protein; 10.4g fibre
tip This recipe is suitable to make in a slow cooker and pressure cooker.

greek-style drumsticks with olives and artichokes

2 tablespoons olive oil
12 chicken drumsticks (1.8kg)
1 medium white onion (150g),
    chopped finely
3 cloves garlic, crushed
1½ cups (375ml)
    chicken stock
½ cup (125ml) dry white wine
340g jar marinated artichokes,
    drained, quartered
2 tablespoons finely grated
    lemon rind
500g risoni
2 tablespoons finely chopped
    fresh oregano
1 cup (150g) seeded
    kalamata olives
¼ cup (60ml) lemon juice

1 Heat half the oil in large heavy-based saucepan; cook chicken, in batches, until browned all over.

2 Heat remaining oil in same pan; cook onion and garlic, stirring, until onion softens. Add stock, wine, artichokes and half the rind; bring to a boil. Return chicken to pan; reduce heat, simmer, covered, 20 minutes. Uncover; simmer about 10 minutes or until drumsticks are cooked through.

3 Meanwhile, cook risoni in large saucepan of boiling water, uncovered, until just tender; drain.

4 Remove chicken from pan. Add oregano, olives, juice and remaining rind to pan juices; stir until heated through.

5 Serve chicken with sauce on risoni.

serves 4
preparation time 15 minutes
cooking time 1 hour
per serving 44.7g total fat (11.7g saturated fat); 4631kJ (1108 cal); 98.7g carbohydrate; 67.8g protein; 5.7g fibre
tips This recipe is not suitable to make in a slow cooker or pressure cooker.
Risoni, also known as risi, is a very small rice-shaped pasta similar to orzo. It is great added to soups, baked in a casserole or as a side dish when served with a main course.

vegetable tagine with lemon couscous

1 tablespoon coriander seeds
1 tablespoon cumin seeds
1 tablespoon caraway seeds
1 tablespoon vegetable oil
3 cloves garlic, crushed
2 large brown onions (400g),
    chopped finely
2 teaspoons sweet paprika
2 teaspoons ground ginger
1 tablespoon tomato paste
2 cups (500ml) water
2 x 425g cans diced tomatoes
600g pumpkin,
    chopped coarsely
8 yellow patty-pan squash
    (240g), quartered
200g baby green beans,
    trimmed, halved
300g can chickpeas,
    rinsed, drained
lemon couscous
2 cups (400g) couscous
2 cups (500ml) boiling water
2 teaspoons coarsely grated
    lemon rind
2 teaspoons lemon juice
2 tablespoons coarsely
    chopped fresh
        flat-leaf parsley

1 Using mortar and pestle, crush seeds to a fine powder. Sift into small bowl; discard husks.
2 Heat oil in large saucepan; cook garlic and onion, stirring, until onion softens. Add crushed seeds and spices; cook, stirring, until fragrant.
3 Add paste, the water, undrained tomatoes and pumpkin; bring to a boil. Reduce heat; simmer, uncovered, 20 minutes. Stir in squash, beans and chickpeas; simmer, covered, about 10 minutes or until squash is tender.
4 Meanwhile, make lemon couscous.
5 Serve tagine with couscous.
lemon couscous Combine couscous with the water in large heatproof bowl; cover, stand about 5 minutes or until water is absorbed, fluffing with fork occasionally. Stir in rind, juice and parsley.

serves 6
preparation time 25 minutes
cooking time 40 minutes
per serving 5g total fat (0.8g saturated fat); 1643kJ (393 cal); 69.9g carbohydrate; 16.2g protein; 7.8g fibre
tip This recipe is not suitable to make in a slow cooker or pressure cooker.

15

lamb shank stew with creamy mash

8 french-trimmed
   lamb shanks (2kg)
8 cloves garlic, halved
2 medium lemons (280g)
2 tablespoons olive oil
3 large brown onions (600g),
   chopped coarsely
2 cups (500ml) dry red wine
3 medium carrots (360g),
   quartered lengthways
3 trimmed celery stalks (300g),
   chopped coarsely
4 bay leaves
8 sprigs fresh thyme
1.75 litres (7 cups)
   chicken stock
½ cup finely chopped
   fresh flat-leaf parsley
¼ cup finely chopped
   fresh mint
2kg potatoes,
   chopped coarsely
300ml cream, warmed
100g butter

1 Preheat oven to 180°C/160°C fan-forced.
2 Pierce meatiest part of each shank in two places with sharp knife; press garlic into cuts.
3 Grate rind of both lemons finely; reserve. Halve lemons; rub cut sides all over shanks.
4 Heat oil in large flameproof casserole dish; cook shanks, in batches, until browned. Add onion to dish; cook, stirring, until softened. Add wine; bring to a boil then remove dish from heat.
5 Place carrot, celery and shanks, in alternate layers, on onion mixture in dish. Top with bay leaves and thyme; carefully pour stock over the top. Cover dish tightly with lid or foil; cook in oven about 3 hours or until meat is tender.
6 Meanwhile, combine reserved grated rind, parsley and mint in small bowl.
7 Cook potato until tender; drain. Mash potato with cream and butter. Cover to keep warm.
8 Transfer shanks to platter; cover to keep warm. Strain pan juices through muslin-lined sieve or colander into medium saucepan; discard solids. Boil pan juices, uncovered, stirring occasionally, until liquid is reduced by half.
9 Divide potato among plates; top with shanks, and lemon-herb mixture, drizzle with pan juices. Serve with steamed green beans, if desired.

preparation time 20 minutes
cooking time 3 hours 20 minutes
serves 8
per serving 34.3g total fat (19.5g saturated fat); 2746kJ (657 cal); 38.3g carbohydrate; 34.3g protein; 7.4g fibre
tip This recipe is suitable to make in a slow cooker and pressure cooker.

cassoulet

1½ cups (300g) dried
 white beans
300g boned pork belly, rind
 removed, sliced thinly
150g piece streaky bacon,
 rind removed, cut into
 1cm pieces
800g piece boned lamb
 shoulder, cut into
 3cm pieces
1 large brown onion (200g),
 chopped finely
1 small leek (200g),
 sliced thinly
2 cloves garlic, crushed
3 sprigs fresh thyme
425g can diced tomatoes
2 bay leaves
1 cup (250ml) water
1 cup (250ml) chicken stock
2 cups (140g) stale
 breadcrumbs
⅓ cup coarsely chopped
 fresh flat-leaf parsley

1 Place beans in medium bowl; cover with water. Stand overnight, drain. Rinse under cold water; drain. Place beans in medium saucepan of boiling water; return to a boil. Reduce heat; simmer, covered, about 15 minutes or until beans are just tender. Drain.
2 Preheat oven to 160°C/140°C fan-forced.
3 Cook pork in large flameproof casserole dish over heat, pressing down with back of spoon on pork until browned all over; remove from dish. Cook bacon in same dish, stirring, until crisp; remove from dish. Cook lamb, in batches, in same dish, until browned all over.
4 Cook onion, leek and garlic in same dish, stirring, until onion softens. Add thyme, undrained tomatoes, bay leaves, the water, stock, beans and meat; bring to a boil. Cover; cook in oven 45 minutes. Remove from oven; sprinkle with combined breadcrumbs and parsley. Return to oven; cook, uncovered, about 45 minutes or until liquid is nearly absorbed and beans are tender.

serves 6
preparation time 40 minutes
(plus standing time)
cooking time 2 hours 10 minutes
per serving 17.1g total fat (6g saturated fat); 2328kJ (557 cal); 39.5g carbohydrate; 54.1g protein; 12g fibre
tip This recipe is suitable to make in a slow cooker and pressure cooker.

lamb and quince tagine with pistachio couscous

40g butter
600g diced lamb
1 medium red onion (170g),
    chopped coarsely
2 cloves garlic, crushed
1 cinnamon stick
2 teaspoons ground coriander
1 teaspoon ground cumin
1 teaspoon ground ginger
1 teaspoon dried chilli flakes
1½ cups (375ml) water
425g can diced tomatoes
2 medium quinces (750g),
    peeled, cored, quartered
1 large zucchini (150g),
    chopped coarsely
2 tablespoons coarsely
    chopped fresh coriander
pistachio couscous
1½ cups (300g) couscous
1 cup (250ml) boiling water
20g butter, softened
½ cup finely chopped
    fresh coriander
¼ cup (35g) roasted pistachios,
    chopped coarsely

1 Melt butter in large saucepan; cook lamb, in batches, until browned. Add onion to same pan; cook, stirring, until softened. Add garlic, cinnamon, ground coriander, cumin, ginger and chilli; cook, stirring, until mixture is fragrant.

2 Return lamb to pan. Stir in the water, undrained tomatoes and quince; bring to a boil. Reduce heat; simmer, covered, 30 minutes. Uncover; simmer, stirring occasionally, about 1 hour or until quince is rosy and tender and sauce has thickened.

3 Add zucchini; cook, stirring, about 10 minutes or until zucchini is just tender.

4 Meanwhile, make couscous.

5 Sprinkle tagine with coriander; serve with couscous.

pistachio couscous Combine couscous with the water and butter in large heatproof bowl, cover; stand about 5 minutes or until water is absorbed, fluffing with fork occasionally. Stir in coriander and nuts.

serves 4
preparation time 20 minutes
cooking time 1 hour 30 minutes
per serving 31g total fat (14.7g saturated fat); 3214kJ (769 cal); 76.7g carbohydrate; 45.4g protein; 12.3g fibre
tip This recipe is suitable to make in a slow cooker and pressure cooker.

beef bourguignon

14 shallots (350g)
2 tablespoons olive oil
2kg gravy beef, trimmed,
 chopped coarsely
30g butter
4 bacon rashers (280g), rind
 removed, chopped coarsely
400g button mushrooms,
 halved
2 cloves garlic, crushed
¼ cup (35g) plain flour
1¼ cups (310ml) beef stock
2½ cups (625ml) dry red wine
2 bay leaves
2 sprigs fresh thyme
½ cup coarsely chopped
 fresh flat-leaf parsley

1 Peel shallots, leaving root end intact so shallot remains whole during cooking.
2 Heat oil in large flameproof casserole dish; cook beef, in batches, until browned.
3 Heat butter in same dish; cook shallots, bacon, mushrooms and garlic, stirring, until shallots are browned lightly.
4 Sprinkle flour over shallot mixture; cook, stirring, until flour mixture thickens and bubbles. Gradually add stock and wine; stir over heat until mixture boils and thickens.
5 Return beef and any juices to dish, add bay leaves and thyme; bring to a boil. Reduce heat; simmer, covered, about 2 hours or until beef is tender, stirring every 30 minutes.
6 Stir in parsley; discard bay leaves just before serving.

serves 6
preparation time 30 minutes
cooking time 2 hours 30 minutes
per serving 27g total fat (10.5g saturated fat); 2750kJ (658 cal); 7.3g carbohydrate; 77.3g protein; 2.8g fibre
tip This recipe is suitable to make in a slow cooker and pressure cooker.

braised beef cheeks in red wine

2 tablespoons olive oil
1.6kg beef cheeks, trimmed
1 medium brown onion (150g),
   chopped coarsely
1 medium carrot (120g),
   chopped coarsely
3 cups (750ml) dry red wine
¼ cup (60ml) red wine vinegar
2 x 425g can diced tomatoes
¼ cup (55g) firmly packed
   brown sugar
1 large fennel bulb (550g),
   cut into thin wedges
2 sprigs fresh rosemary
6 black peppercorns
2 tablespoons fresh
   oregano leaves
400g spring onions,
   trimmed, halved
200g swiss brown mushrooms
cheesy polenta
2⅓ cups (580ml) water
2⅓ cups (580ml) milk
1 cup (170g) polenta
½ cup (40g) finely grated
   parmesan cheese
30g butter

1 Preheat oven to 160°C/140°C fan-forced.
2 Heat half the oil in large flameproof casserole dish; cook beef, in batches, until browned all over.
3 Heat remaining oil in same dish; cook brown onion and carrot, stirring, until onion softens. Return beef to dish with wine, vinegar, undrained tomatoes, sugar, fennel, rosemary, peppercorns and oregano; bring to a boil. Cover; cook in oven 2 hours.
4 Stir in spring onion and mushrooms; cook, uncovered, in oven about 45 minutes or until beef is tender.
5 Meanwhile, make cheesy polenta; serve with beef.

cheesy polenta Combine the water and milk in large saucepan; bring to a boil. Gradually add polenta to liquid, stirring constantly. Reduce heat; simmer, stirring, about 10 minutes or until polenta thickens. Stir in cheese and butter.

serves 4
preparation time 20 minutes
cooking time 3 hours 10 minutes
per serving 39.8g total fat (16.2g saturated fat); 4828kJ (1155 cal); 67.1g carbohydrate; 100.8g protein; 10.3g fibre
tips You may need to preorder the beef cheeks from your butcher.
This recipe is suitable to make in a slow cooker and pressure cooker.

beef and prune tagine
with spinach couscous

2 large red onions (600g),
   chopped finely
2 tablespoons olive oil
1 teaspoon cracked
   black pepper
pinch saffron threads
1 teaspoon ground cinnamon
¼ teaspoon ground ginger
1kg beef blade steak, diced
   into 4cm pieces
50g butter, chopped
425g can diced tomatoes
1 cup (250ml) water
2 tablespoons white sugar
¾ cup (100g) roasted
   slivered almonds
1½ cups (250g)
   seeded prunes
1 teaspoon finely grated
   lemon rind
¼ teaspoon ground
   cinnamon, extra

spinach couscous
1½ cups (300g) couscous
1½ cups (375ml) boiling water
80g baby spinach leaves,
   shredded finely

1 Combine onion, oil, pepper, saffron, cinnamon and ginger in large bowl; add beef, toss beef to coat in mixture.

2 Place beef in large deep saucepan with butter, undrained tomatoes, the water, half the sugar and ½ cup of the nuts; bring to a boil. Reduce heat; simmer, covered, 1½ hours. Remove 1 cup cooking liquid; reserve. Simmer tagine, uncovered, 30 minutes.

3 Meanwhile, place prunes in small bowl, cover with boiling water; stand 20 minutes, drain. Place prunes in small saucepan with rind, extra cinnamon, remaining sugar and reserved cooking liquid; bring to a boil. Reduce heat; simmer, uncovered, about 15 minutes or until prunes soften. Stir into tagine.

4 Make spinach couscous.

5 Divide couscous and tagine among serving plates; sprinkle with remaining nuts.

spinach couscous Combine couscous with the boiling water in large heatproof bowl, cover; stand about 5 minutes or until water is absorbed, fluffing with fork occasionally. Stir in spinach.

serves 4
preparation time 20 minutes
cooking time 2 hours 30 minutes
per serving 50.3g total fat (16.5g saturated fat); 4799kJ (1148 cal); 102.3g carbohydrate; 72.1g protein; 11.6g fibre
tip This recipe is suitable to make in a slow cooker and pressure cooker.

osso buco with caper gremolata

8 pieces veal osso buco (2kg)
2 tablespoons plain flour
¼ cup (60ml) olive oil
1 medium brown onion (150g),
    chopped coarsely
2 cloves garlic, crushed
3 trimmed celery stalks (300g),
    chopped coarsely
2 large carrots (360g),
    chopped coarsely
2 x 425g can diced tomatoes
2 tablespoons tomato paste
1 cup (250ml) dry white wine
1 cup (250ml) beef stock
3 sprigs fresh thyme
caper gremolata
1 tablespoon finely grated
    lemon rind
⅓ cup finely chopped fresh
    flat-leaf parsley
2 cloves garlic, chopped finely
1 tablespoon drained capers,
    rinsed, chopped finely

1 Toss veal in flour; shake away excess. Heat 2 tablespoons of the oil in large flameproof casserole dish; cook veal, in batches, until browned all over.
2 Heat remaining oil in same dish; cook onion, garlic, celery and carrot, stirring, until vegetables soften. Stir in undrained tomatoes, tomato paste, wine, stock and thyme.
3 Return veal to dish, fitting pieces upright and tightly together in single layer; bring to a boil. Reduce heat; simmer, covered, 2 hours. Uncover; cook about 30 minutes or until veal is almost falling off the bone.
4 Meanwhile, make caper gremolata.
5 Divide veal among serving plates; top with sauce, sprinkle with gremolata. Serve with soft polenta, if desired.
caper gremolata Combine ingredients in small bowl.

serves 4
preparation time 25 minutes
cooking time 2 hours
per serving 19.9g total fat (4.4g saturated fat); 2240kJ (536 cal); 13.2g carbohydrate; 68.7g protein; 5.3g fibre
tip This recipe is suitable to make in a slow cooker and pressure cooker.

fish in spicy coconut cream

2 teaspoons peanut oil
2 cloves garlic, crushed
1cm piece fresh ginger
(5g), grated
20g piece fresh turmeric,
grated finely
2 fresh small red thai chillies,
sliced thinly
1½ cups (375ml) fish stock
400ml can coconut cream
4cm piece fresh galangal
(20g), halved
10cm stick fresh lemon grass
(20g), cut into 2cm pieces
4 firm white fish fillets (800g)
2 tablespoons fish sauce
2 green onions, sliced thinly

1 Heat oil in wok; stir-fry garlic, ginger, turmeric and chilli until fragrant. Add stock, coconut cream, galangal and lemon grass; bring to a boil. Add fish, reduce heat; simmer, covered, about 8 minutes or until fish is cooked.

2 Using slotted spoon, remove fish carefully from liquid; place in serving bowl, cover to keep warm. Remove and discard galangal and lemon grass pieces from liquid. Bring liquid to a boil; boil 5 minutes. Remove from heat; stir in sauce and onion. Pour sauce over fish in bowl.

serves 4
preparation time 20 minutes
cooking time 30 minutes
per serving 27.7g total fat (0.8g saturated fat); 915kJ (219 cal); 26.3g carbohydrate; 15.3g protein; 11.2g fibre
tip This recipe is not suitable to make in a slow cooker or pressure cooker.

ling and snow pea green curry

1¼ cups (250g) jasmine rice
2 teaspoons peanut oil
1 medium brown onion (150g),
   chopped finely
3 small green chillies,
   sliced thinly
¼ cup (75g) prepared green
   curry paste
1⅔ cups (400ml) coconut milk
4 ling fillets (800g), skinned,
   chopped coarsely
200g snow peas, halved
4 green onions, sliced thinly
¼ cup coarsely chopped
   fresh coriander

1 Cook rice in large saucepan of boiling water, uncovered, until tender; drain, cover to keep warm.

2 Meanwhile, heat oil in large saucepan; cook brown onion, chilli and curry paste, stirring, until onion softens. Stir in coconut milk; bring to a boil. Add fish, reduce heat; simmer, uncovered, 5 minutes. Add snow peas and green onion; stir gently until vegetables are just tender. Remove from heat; stir in half the coriander.

3 Sprinkle curry with remaining coriander; serve with rice.

serves 4
preparation time 30 minutes
cooking time 15 minutes
per serving 30.5g total fat
(19.4g saturated fat); 2997kJ (717 cal);
59.3g carbohydrate; 48.6g protein; 6g fibre
tip This recipe is not suitable to make in
a slow cooker or pressure cooker.

chicken green curry

¼ cup (75g) prepared green
curry paste
2 x 400ml cans coconut milk
2 fresh kaffir lime leaves, torn
2 tablespoons peanut oil
1kg chicken thigh fillets,
trimmed, quartered
2 tablespoons fish sauce
2 tablespoons lime juice
1 tablespoon grated
palm sugar
150g pea eggplants,
quartered
1 small zucchini (90g), cut
into 5cm pieces
⅓ cup loosely packed thai
basil leaves
¼ cup coarsely chopped
fresh coriander
1 tablespoon fresh
coriander leaves
1 long green thai chilli,
sliced thinly
2 green onions, sliced thinly

1 Place curry paste in large saucepan;
stir over heat until fragrant. Add coconut
milk and lime leaves, bring to a boil. Reduce
heat; simmer, stirring, 5 minutes.
2 Meanwhile, heat oil in large frying pan; cook
chicken, in batches, until just browned. Drain
on absorbent paper.
3 Add chicken, sauce, juice, sugar and
eggplant to curry mixture; simmer, covered,
about 5 minutes or until eggplant is tender
and chicken is cooked through. Add zucchini,
basil and chopped coriander; cook, stirring,
until zucchini is just tender.
4 Serve curry sprinkled with coriander leaves,
chilli and onion.

serves 4
preparation time 20 minutes
cooking time 20 minutes
per serving 67.1g total fat (41.6g saturated fat);
3775kJ (9.3 cal); 14.5g carbohydrate;
58.5g protein; 7.1g fibre
tip This recipe is not suitable to make in
a slow cooker or pressure cooker.

thai red chicken curry

2 cups (400g) jasmine rice
2 tablespoons peanut oil
750g chicken thigh fillets,
    chopped coarsely
1 large brown onion (200g),
    chopped coarsely
3 cloves garlic, crushed
2 tablespoons prepared
    red curry paste
1 fresh long red chilli, halved
    lengthways, sliced thinly
1 teaspoon ground cumin
3 baby eggplants (180g),
    sliced thickly
1 tablespoon fish sauce
3 fresh kaffir lime leaves,
    sliced thinly
140ml can coconut milk
¾ cup (180ml) water
150g snake beans, cut into
    5cm lengths
⅓ cup loosely packed fresh
    coriander leaves

1 Cook rice in large saucepan of boiling water, uncovered, until just tender; drain.
2 Meanwhile, heat half the oil in wok; stir-fry chicken, in batches, until browned.
3 Heat remaining oil in wok; stir-fry onion and garlic until onion softens. Add paste, chilli and cumin; stir-fry until fragrant. Add eggplant; stir-fry until browned lightly.
4 Return chicken to wok with sauce, lime leaves, coconut milk, the water and beans; stir-fry about 5 minutes or until chicken is cooked through and sauce is thickened slightly.
5 Serve curry and rice sprinkled with coriander.

serves 4
preparation time 15 minutes
cooking time 30 minutes
per serving 34.4g total fat (12.6g saturated fat); 3557kJ (851 cal); 86.8g carbohydrate; 46g protein; 6g fibre
tips This recipe is not suitable to make in a slow cooker or pressure cooker.
You'll need half a bunch of snake beans for this recipe.

butter chicken

1 cup (150g) unsalted
  raw cashews
2 teaspoons garam masala
2 teaspoons ground coriander
½ teaspoon chilli powder
3 cloves garlic,
  chopped coarsely
4cm piece fresh ginger
  (20g), grated
2 tablespoons white vinegar
⅓ cup (90g) tomato paste
½ cup (140g) yogurt
1kg chicken thigh
  fillets, halved
80g butter
1 large brown onion (200g),
  chopped finely
1 cinnamon stick
4 cardamom pods, bruised
1 teaspoon hot paprika
400g can tomato puree
¾ cup (180ml) chicken stock
¾ cup (180ml) cream

1 Dry-fry nuts, garam masala, coriander and chilli in small frying pan, stirring, until nuts are browned lightly.

2 Blend or process nut mixture with garlic, ginger, vinegar, paste and half the yogurt until mixture forms a paste. Transfer to large bowl; stir in remaining yogurt and chicken. Cover; refrigerate 3 hours or overnight.

3 Melt butter in large saucepan; cook onion, cinnamon and cardamom, stirring, until onion is browned lightly. Add chicken mixture; cook, stirring, 10 minutes.

4 Stir in paprika, puree and stock; simmer, uncovered, 45 minutes, stirring occasionally.

5 Discard cinnamon and cardamom. Add cream; simmer, uncovered, 5 minutes.

serves 4
preparation time 30 minutes
(plus refrigeration time)
cooking time 1 hour 10 minutes
per serving 74g total fat (33.3g saturated fat); 4138kJ (990 cal); 20.8g carbohydrate; 59.3g protein; 6.5g fibre

tips This recipe is not suitable to make in a slow cooker or pressure cooker.
Use unsalted cashews in the roasted curry mixture or the taste of the finished butter chicken may not be as mellow as it could be.

chicken panang curry

2 x 400ml cans coconut milk
¼ cup (75g) prepared panang
  curry paste
2 tablespoons grated
  palm sugar
2 tablespoons fish sauce
2 fresh kaffir lime leaves, torn
2 tablespoons peanut oil
1kg chicken thigh fillets,
  quartered
100g snake beans,
  chopped coarsely
½ cup firmly packed thai
  basil leaves
½ cup (70g) coarsely chopped
  roasted unsalted peanuts
2 fresh long red chillies,
  sliced thinly

1 Place coconut milk, paste, sugar, sauce and lime leaves in wok; bring to a boil, reduce heat. Simmer, stirring, about 15 minutes or until mixture reduces by about a third.
2 Meanwhile, heat oil in large frying pan; cook chicken, in batches, until browned lightly. Drain on absorbent paper.
3 Add beans, chicken and half the basil to curry mixture; cook, uncovered, stirring occasionally, about 5 minutes or until beans are just tender and chicken is cooked through.
4 Serve curry sprinkled with peanuts, chilli and remaining basil.

serves 4
preparation time 15 minutes
cooking time 20 minutes
per serving 75g total fat (42.8g saturated fat); 4197kJ (1004 cal); 17.8g carbohydrate; 62.6g protein; 7.7g fibre
tip This recipe is not suitable to make in a slow cooker or pressure cooker.

massaman curry

1kg beef skirt steak, cut into
　3cm pieces
2 cups (500ml) beef stock
2 star anise
5 cardamom pods, bruised
¼ teaspoon ground clove
1 tablespoon grated
　palm sugar
2 tablespoons fish sauce
2 tablespoons tamarind
　concentrate
2 x 400ml cans coconut milk
2 tablespoons prepared
　massaman curry paste
8 baby brown onions
　(200g), halved
1 medium kumara (400g),
　chopped coarsely
¼ cup (35g) coarsely chopped
　roasted unsalted peanuts
2 green onions, sliced thinly

1 Place beef, 1½ cups of the stock, star anise, cardamom, clove, sugar, sauce, 1 tablespoon of tamarind and half the coconut milk in large saucepan; simmer, uncovered, about 1½ hours or until beef is almost tender.

2 Strain beef over large bowl; reserve 1 cup of the braising liquid, discard solids. Cover beef to keep warm.

3 Cook curry paste in same pan, stirring, until fragrant. Add remaining coconut milk, tamarind and stock; bring to a boil. Cook, stirring, about 1 minute or until mixture is smooth. Return beef to pan with brown onion, kumara and the reserved braising liquid; simmer, uncovered, about 30 minutes or until beef and vegetables are tender.

4 Stir nuts and green onion into curry off the heat.

serves 4
preparation time 20 minutes
cooking time 2 hours 10 minutes
per serving 52.7g total fat (39.5g saturated fat); 3645kJ (872 cal); 29.2g carbohydrate; 67.4g protein; 7.2g fibre
tip This recipe is suitable to make in a slow cooker and pressure cooker.

xacutti

Xacutti (pronounced sha-koo-tee) is a Goan curry, traditionally made with mutton or chicken and a dry curry paste containing fried coconut; it has lime juice added just before serving.

1 cup (80g) desiccated coconut

½ teaspoon ground cinnamon

4 whole cloves

8 dried long red chillies

1 teaspoon ground turmeric

1 tablespoon poppy seeds

1 tablespoon cumin seeds

1 tablespoon fennel seeds

2 tablespoons coriander seeds

2 teaspoons black peppercorns

2 star anise

6 cloves garlic, quartered

2 tablespoons ghee

1 large brown onion (200g), chopped finely

1kg diced beef rump

2 cups (500ml) water

2 cups (500ml) beef stock

2 tablespoons lime juice

1 Dry-fry coconut in large frying pan over medium heat, stirring, until browned lightly; remove coconut from pan. Dry-fry cinnamon, cloves, chillies, turmeric, seeds, peppercorns and star anise in same pan, stirring, about 1 minute or until fragrant.

2 Blend or process coconut, spice mixture and garlic until fine.

3 Heat ghee in large saucepan; cook onion, stirring, until soft. Add coconut spice mixture; cook, stirring, until fragrant. Add beef; cook, stirring, about 2 minutes or until beef is coated with coconut spice mixture.

4 Add the water and stock; simmer, covered, 30 minutes, stirring occasionally. Uncover; cook 30 minutes or until beef is tender and sauce thickens slightly. Stir juice into curry off the heat; sprinkle with fresh sliced chilli, if desired.

serves 4
preparation time 25 minutes
cooking time 1 hour 15 minutes
per serving 38.2g total fat (23.8g saturated fat); 2512kJ (600 cal); 5g carbohydrate; 57.5g protein; 5.2g fibre
tip This recipe is suitable to make in a slow cooker and pressure cooker.

rogan josh

1 tablespoon vegetable oil

1kg lamb shoulder, diced into
   3cm pieces

3 medium brown onions
   (450g), sliced thinly

4cm piece fresh ginger
   (20g), grated

2 cloves garlic, crushed

⅔ cup (200g) prepared
   rogan josh paste

1½ cups (375ml) water

425g can diced tomatoes

1 cinnamon stick

5 cardamom pods, bruised

2 tablespoons coarsely
   chopped fresh coriander

1 Heat half the oil in large saucepan; cook lamb, in batches, until browned.

2 Heat remaining oil in same pan; cook onion, stirring, until soft. Add ginger, garlic and paste; cook, stirring, until fragrant.

3 Return lamb to pan; stir to combine with paste mixture. Add the water, undrained tomatoes, cinnamon and cardamom; simmer, covered, about 1½ hours or until lamb is tender. Serve curry sprinkled with coriander.

serves 6

preparation time 25 minutes

cooking time 1 hour 50 minutes

per serving 28.6g total fat (8.3g saturated fat); 1835kJ (439 cal); 7.8g carbohydrate; 35.7g protein; 5.5g fibre

tip This recipe is suitable to make in a slow cooker and pressure cooker.

lamb korma

⅓ cup (55g) blanched
   almonds
3 tablespoons ghee
800g lamb strips
1 large brown onion
   (200g), sliced thinly
2 cloves garlic, crushed
4cm piece fresh ginger
   (20g), grated
2 teaspoons
   poppy seeds
½ cup (150g) prepared
   korma paste
½ cup (125ml)
   chicken stock
300ml cream
⅓ cup (95g) yogurt

1 Blend or process nuts until finely ground.
2 Heat 2 tablespoons of ghee in large saucepan; cook lamb, in batches, until browned.
3 Heat remaining ghee in same pan; cook onion, garlic and ginger, stirring, until onion softens. Add ground nuts, seeds and paste; cook, stirring, until fragrant.
4 Return lamb to pan with stock and cream; simmer, uncovered, about 15 minutes or until sauce thickens slightly. Serve korma accompanied by yogurt.

serves 4
preparation time 25 minutes
(plus refrigeration time)
cooking time 40 minutes
per serving 84.1g total fat (40.3g saturated fat); 4172kJ (998 cal); 9.2g carbohydrate; 50.6g protein; 6.4g fibre
tip This recipe is not suitable to make in a slow cooker or pressure cooker.

sour pork curry

1 tablespoon vegetable oil
1kg pork neck
1 teaspoon shrimp paste
¼ cup coarsely chopped
    coriander root and
    stem mixture
2cm piece fresh galangal
    (10g), chopped finely
5 dried long red chillies,
    chopped finely
3 fresh long red chillies,
    chopped finely
2 tablespoons fish sauce
¾ cup (235g) tamarind
    concentrate
2 tablespoons caster sugar
2 cups (500ml) chicken stock
1 litre (4 cups) water
½ cup thai basil leaves,
    chopped coarsely

1 Heat oil in large flameproof casserole dish, add pork; cook, uncovered, until browned. Remove from dish.
2 Preheat oven to 160°C/140°C fan-forced.
3 Add paste, coriander mixture, galangal and chillies to same dish; cook, stirring, until fragrant. Add sauce, tamarind, sugar, stock and the water; bring to a boil. Return pork to dish, cover; cook in oven 1 hour. Uncover; cook 1 hour.
4 Remove pork from dish, cover; stand 10 minutes before slicing thickly. Stir basil into curry sauce off the heat.

serves 4
preparation time 30 minutes
cooking time 2 hours 15 minutes
per serving 9.3g total fat (2.1g saturated fat); 1680kJ (402 cal); 18.3g carbohydrate; 59.7g protein; 1.5g fibre
tips This recipe is suitable to make in a slow cooker and pressure cooker. When purchasing coriander, make sure you buy stems that also have the root attached for this recipe. Wash well before using.

pork vindaloo

2 tablespoons ghee
1kg pork shoulder, cut into 3cm pieces
1 large red onion (300g), sliced thinly
½ cup (150g) prepared vindaloo paste
2 cloves garlic, crushed
2 cups (500ml) water
¼ cup (60ml) white vinegar
4 medium potatoes (800g), quartered
2 fresh small red thai chillies, chopped finely
2 fresh long red chillies, sliced thinly

1 Heat ghee in large saucepan; cook pork, in batches, until browned all over.
2 Cook onion in same pan, stirring, until soft. Add paste and garlic; cook, stirring, about 1 minute or until fragrant.
3 Return pork to pan with the water and vinegar; simmer, covered, 50 minutes.
4 Add potato; simmer, uncovered, about 45 minutes or until potato is tender. Stir in chopped chilli; serve curry sprinkled with thinly sliced chilli.

serves 4
preparation time 25 minutes
cooking time 1 hour 50 minutes
per serving 40.7g total fat (13.7g saturated fat); 3173kJ (759 cal); 33.3g carbohydrate; 61g protein; 8.3g fibre
tip This recipe is suitable to make in a slow cooker and pressure cooker.

cauliflower and green pea curry

600g cauliflower florets
2 tablespoons ghee
1 medium brown onion (150g),
    chopped finely
2 cloves garlic, crushed
2cm piece fresh ginger
    (10g), grated
¼ cup (75g) prepared
    hot curry paste
¾ cup (180ml) cream
2 large tomatoes (440g),
    chopped coarsely
1 cup (120g) frozen peas
1 cup (280g) yogurt
¼ cup finely chopped
    fresh coriander
3 hard-boiled eggs,
    sliced thinly

1 Boil, steam or microwave cauliflower until just tender; drain.

2 Meanwhile, heat ghee in large saucepan; cook onion, garlic and ginger, stirring, until onion softens. Add paste; cook, stirring, until mixture is fragrant.

3 Add cream; bring to a boil then reduce heat. Add cauliflower and tomato; simmer, uncovered, 5 minutes, stirring occasionally.

4 Add peas and yogurt; stir over low heat about 5 minutes or until peas are just cooked. Serve curry with egg and sprinkled with coriander.

serves 4
preparation time 20 minutes
cooking time 30 minutes
per serving 40.9g total fat (21.9g saturated fat); 2132kJ (510 cal); 15.5g carbohydrate; 17g protein; 8.6g fibre
tips This recipe is not suitable to make in a slow cooker or pressure cooker. Cauliflower is a popular choice for vegetarian curries because it's both filling and, while it has a great taste of its own, the texture of the florets captures the sauce. In this recipe we used vindaloo paste, but any hot curry paste (red curry paste, for example) would work just as well.

tofu and vegetable yellow curry

1⅔ cups (400ml) light
    coconut milk
1 cup (250ml) vegetable stock
1 large kumara (500g),
    chopped coarsely
200g green beans, trimmed
150g firm tofu, cut into
    2cm cubes
2 tablespoons lime juice
¼ cup coarsely chopped
    fresh coriander
2 cups (400g) jasmine rice
yellow curry paste
1 teaspoon ground coriander
1 teaspoon ground cumin
1 teaspoon ground cinnamon
4cm piece fresh ginger (20g),
    chopped coarsely
2 cloves garlic, quartered
5 fresh long red chillies,
    chopped coarsely
5cm stick fresh lemon grass
    (10g), coarsely chopped
3 green onions,
    chopped finely
1 teaspoon salt
2 teaspoons curry powder
1 medium brown onion (150g),
    chopped coarsely

1 Make yellow curry paste.
2 Cook half the curry paste in large saucepan, stirring, until fragrant. Add coconut milk and stock; bring to a boil. Reduce heat; simmer, stirring, 5 minutes. Add kumara; simmer, covered, about 10 minutes or until kumara is tender. Add beans, tofu and juice; cook, stirring, until beans are tender. Stir in coriander.
3 Meanwhile, cook rice in large saucepan of boiling water, uncovered, until just tender; drain.
4 Sprinkle curry with extra fresh coriander, if desired; serve with rice.

yellow curry paste Dry-fry coriander, cumin and cinnamon in small frying pan, stirring, until fragrant. Blend or process spices with remaining ingredients until mixture forms a paste.

serves 4
preparation time 20 minutes
cooking time 30 minutes
per serving 3.5g total fat (3.5g saturated fat); 518kJ (124 cal); 20g carbohydrate; 3.4g protein; 1.2g fibre
tips This recipe is not suitable to make in a slow cooker or pressure cooker.
Any leftover curry paste can be frozen for up to three months. Place tablespoons of paste in an ice-cube tray, wrap tightly in plastic wrap and freeze.

coconut fish curry

¼ cup (60ml) vegetable oil
800g firm white fish fillets,
  cut into 3cm pieces
1 medium brown onion (150g),
  sliced thinly
2 cloves garlic, crushed
2 long green chillies,
  sliced thinly
3 teaspoons garam masala
1⅔ cups (400ml) coconut milk
2 tablespoons lemon juice
¼ cup (60ml) tamarind
  concentrate
1 large tomato (220g),
  chopped coarsely
1 medium red capsicum (200g),
  chopped coarsely
⅓ cup firmly packed fresh
  coriander leaves
1 medium lemon (140g), cut
  into wedges

1 Heat 2 tablespoons of the oil in large saucepan; cook fish, in batches, until browned all over.
2 Heat remaining oil in same pan; cook onion, garlic and half the chilli, stirring, until onion softens. Add garam masala; cook, stirring, until fragrant. Add coconut milk, juice, tamarind, tomato and capsicum; bring to a boil. Add fish, reduce heat; simmer, covered, about 5 minutes or until fish is cooked as desired.
3 Divide curry among serving bowls; top with coriander and remaining chilli. Serve with lemon wedges, and naan, if desired.

serves 4
preparation time 25 minutes
cooking time 20 minutes
per serving 36.5g total fat (20.6g saturated fat); 2257kJ (540 cal); 9.1g carbohydrate; 43.7g protein; 4.6g fibre
tips This recipe is not suitable to make in a slow cooker or pressure cooker.
We used ling in this recipe, but you can use any firm white fish fillet such as perch or blue-eye fillets.

glossary

bacon rashers also known as bacon slices; made from cured and smoked pork side.

beans, snake long (about 40cm), thin, round, fresh green beans; Asian in origin, with a taste similar to green or french beans. They are also called yard-long beans because of their length.

butter use salted or unsalted (sweet) butter; 125g is equal to one stick of butter.

capers the grey-green buds of a warm climate (usually Mediterranean) shrub, sold either dried and salted or pickled in a vinegar brine; tiny young ones, called baby capers, are also available both in brine or dried in salt.

capsicum also known as pepper or bell pepper.

cheese
  parmesan also known as parmigiano, parmesan is a hard, grainy cow-milk cheese that originated in the Parma region of Italy.
  ricotta a soft, sweet, moist, white cow-milk cheese with a low fat content and a slightly grainy texture.

chickpeas also called channa, garbanzos or hummus; a sandy-coloured, irregularly round legume.

cinnamon dried inner bark of the shoots of the cinnamon tree; available in stick or ground form. Used in both sweet and savoury dishes.

clove dried flower buds of a tropical tree; can be used whole or in ground form. They have a strong scent and taste, so use sparingly.

coriander also known as cilantro, pak chee or chinese parsley; bright-green-leafed herb having both pungent aroma and taste.

couscous a fine, grain-like cereal product made from semolina.

cumin also known as zeera or comino; the dried seed of a plant related to the parsley family. Has a spicy, almost curry-like, flavour.

eggplant also known as aubergine.
  baby also known as finger or japanese eggplant.
  pea about the size of a pea; also known as makeua puan. Sold in clusters of 10 to 15 eggplants; very bitter in flavour, and suit rich, sweet coconut-sauced curries. Found in Asian greengrocers fresh or pickled.

fennel also known as anise or finocchio; a crunchy green vegetable slightly resembling celery. Also the name given to the dried seeds, which have a stronger licorice flavour.

fish sauce made from pulverised salted fermented fish (most often anchovies); has a pungent smell and strong taste, so use according to your taste.

galangal also known as ka or lengkaus if fresh, and laos if dried and powdered; a root, similar to ginger in its use. It has a hot-sour ginger-citrusy flavour.

garam masala meaning blended spices; based on varying proportions of cardamom, cinnamon, cloves, coriander, fennel and cumin, roasted and ground together.

ghee clarified butter; has had the milk solids removed. Has a high smoking point so can be heated to a high temperature without burning.

kaffir lime leaves also known as bai magrood; look like two glossy dark green leaves joined end to end, forming a rounded hourglass shape. A strip of fresh lime peel may be substituted for each kaffir lime leaf.

kumara an orange-fleshed sweet potato often confused with yam.

lemon grass also known as takrai, serai or serah. A tall, clumping, lemon-smelling and tasting, sharp-edged aromatic tropical grass; the white lower part of the stem is used, finely chopped.

onion
  green also known as scallion or (incorrectly) shallot; an immature onion picked before the bulb has formed, having a long, bright-green edible stalk.

red also known as spanish, red spanish or bermuda onion; a sweet-flavoured, large, purple-red onion.

paprika ground dried sweet red capsicum (bell pepper); there are many grades and types available, including sweet, hot, mild and smoked.

parsley, flat-leaf also known as continental or Italian parsley.

patty-pan squash also known as crookneck or custard marrow pumpkins; a round, slightly flat, yellow to pale green squash having a scalloped edge. Harvested young, it has firm white flesh and a distinct flavour.

pine nuts also known as pignoli; not, in fact, a nut but a small, cream-coloured kernel from pine cones.

pistachio green, delicately flavoured nuts inside hard off-white shells.

polenta also known as cornmeal; a flour-like cereal made of dried corn (maize). Also the name of the dish made from it.

prawns also known as shrimp.

prosciutto a kind of unsmoked Italian ham; salted, air-cured and aged, it is usually eaten uncooked.

quince yellow-skinned fruit with a hard texture and an astringent, tart taste; eaten cooked or as a preserve. Long, slow cooking makes the flesh a deep rose pink.

rice, jasmine a long-grained white rice recognised around the world as having a perfumed aromatic quality; moist in texture, it clings together after cooking.

risoni also known as risi; is a very small rice-shaped pasta similar to orzo.

saffron stigma of a member of the crocus family, available ground or in strands; imparts a yellow-orange colour to food once infused. The quality can vary greatly; the best is the most expensive spice in the world.

shallots also called french shallots, golden shallots or eschalots. Small, elongated, brown-skinned members of the onion family; grows in tight clusters similar to garlic.

shrimp paste also known as kapi, trasi and blanchan; a strong-scented, very firm preserved paste made of salted dried shrimp; should be used sparingly. It should be chopped or sliced thinly then wrapped in foil and roasted before use.

spinach also known as english spinach and, incorrectly, silver beet. Baby spinach leaves are also available.

star anise a dried star-shaped fruit of a tree native to China. The pods, which have an astringent aniseed or licorice flavour, are used to flavour stocks and marinades.

sugar
  brown finely granulated, soft sugar retaining molasses for its characteristic colour and flavour.
  palm also known as nam tan pip, jaggery, jawa or gula melaka; made from the sap of the sugar palm tree. Light brown to black in colour and usually sold in rock-hard cakes; substitute with brown sugar, if unavailable.
  white granulated table sugar, also known as crystal sugar.

tamarind concentrate (or paste) the commercial result of the distillation of tamarind juice into a condensed, compacted paste.

tofu also known as soybean curd or bean curd; an off-white, custard-like product made from the "milk" of crushed soybeans.

turmeric also known as kamin; is a rhizome related to galangal and ginger. Must be grated or pounded to release its somewhat acrid aroma and pungent flavour.

white beans a generic term we use for canned or dried cannellini, haricot, navy or great northern beans.

zucchini also known as courgette; small, pale- or dark-green, yellow or white vegetable belonging to the squash family. The young plant has edible flowers that can be stuffed then deep-fried or oven-baked.

conversion chart

MEASURES

One Australian metric measuring cup holds approximately 250ml, one Australian metric tablespoon holds 20ml, one Australian metric teaspoon holds 5ml.

The difference between one country's measuring cups and another's is within a 2- or 3-teaspoon variance, and will not affect your cooking results. North America, New Zealand and the United Kingdom use a 15ml tablespoon. All cup and spoon measurements are level. The most accurate way of measuring dry ingredients is to weigh them. When measuring liquids, use a clear glass or plastic jug with metric markings.

We use large eggs with an average weight of 60g.

DRY MEASURES

METRIC	IMPERIAL
15g	½oz
30g	1oz
60g	2oz
90g	3oz
125g	4oz (¼lb)
155g	5oz
185g	6oz
220g	7oz
250g	8oz (½lb)
280g	9oz
315g	10oz
345g	11oz
375g	12oz (¾lb)
410g	13oz
440g	14oz
470g	15oz
500g	16oz (1lb)
750g	24oz (1½lb)
1kg	32oz (2lb)

LIQUID MEASURES

METRIC	IMPERIAL
30ml	1 fluid oz
60ml	2 fluid oz
100ml	3 fluid oz
125ml	4 fluid oz
150ml	5 fluid oz (¼ pint/1 gill)
190ml	6 fluid oz
250ml	8 fluid oz
300ml	10 fluid oz (½ pint)
500ml	16 fluid oz
600ml	20 fluid oz (1 pint)
1000ml (1 litre)	1¾ pints

LENGTH MEASURES

METRIC	IMPERIAL
3mm	⅛in
6mm	¼in
1cm	½in
2cm	¾in
2.5cm	1in
5cm	2in
6cm	2½in
8cm	3in
10cm	4in
13cm	5in
15cm	6in
18cm	7in
20cm	8in
23cm	9in
25cm	10in
28cm	11in
30cm	12in (1ft)

OVEN TEMPERATURES

These oven temperatures are only a guide for conventional ovens. For fan-forced ovens, check the manufacturer's manual.

	°C (CELSIUS)	°F (FAHRENHEIT)	GAS MARK
Very slow	120	250	½
Slow	150	275 – 300	1 – 2
Moderately slow	160	325	3
Moderate	180	350 – 375	4 – 5
Moderately hot	200	400	6
Hot	220	425 – 450	7 – 8
Very hot	240	475	9

Are you missing some of the world's favourite cookbooks?

The Australian Women's Weekly cookbooks are available from bookshops, cookshops, supermarkets and other stores all over the world. You can also buy direct from the publisher, using the order form below.

MINI SERIES £3.50 190x138MM 64 PAGES

TITLE	QTY	TITLE	QTY	TITLE	QTY
4 Fast Ingredients		Finger Food		Potatoes	
15-minute Feasts		Fishcakes & Crispybakes		Quick Desserts (Mar 08)	
50 Fast Chicken Fillets		Grills & Barbecues		Roast	
50 Fast Desserts		Gluten-free Cooking		Salads	
After-work Stir-fries		Healthy Everyday Food 4 Kids		Simple Slices	
Barbecue Chicken		Ice-creams & Sorbets		Simply Seafood	
Bites		Indian Cooking		Skinny Food	
Bowl Food		Italian Favourites		Spanish Favourites	
Burgers, Rösti & Fritters		Jams & Jellies		Stir-fry Favourites	
Cafe Cakes		Japanese Favourites		Stir-fries	
Cafe Food		Kebabs & Skewers		Summer Salads	
Casseroles		Kids Party Food		Tagines & Couscous	
Casseroles & Curries		Last-minute Meals		Tapas, Antipasto & Mezze	
Char-grills & Barbecues		Lebanese Cooking		Tarts	
Cheesecakes, Pavlova & Trifles		Low-Fat Delicious		Tex-Mex	
Chinese Favourites		Malaysian Favourites		Thai Favourites	
Christmas Cakes & Puddings		Mince		The Fast Egg	
Cocktails		Mince Favourites		Vegetarian	
Crumbles & Bakes		Muffins		Vegie Main Meals	
Cupcakes & Cookies		Noodles		Vietnamese Favourites	
Curries		Noodles & Stir-fries		Wok	
Dips & Dippers		Outdoor Eating			
Dried Fruit & Nuts		Party Food			
Drinks		Pickles and Chutneys			
Easy Pies & Pastries		Pasta		TOTAL COST £	

Photocopy and complete coupon below

Name _____

Address _____

_____ Postcode _____

Country _____ Phone (business hours) _____

Email*(optional) _____
* By including your email address, you consent to receipt of any email regarding this magazine, and other emails which inform you of ACP's other publications, products, services and events, and to promote third party goods and services you may be interested in.

I enclose my cheque/money order for £ _____ or please charge £ _____
to my: ☐ Access ☐ Mastercard ☐ Visa ☐ Diners Club

Card number | | | | | | | | | | | | | | | |

3 digit security code *(found on reverse of card)* _____

Cardholder's signature _____ Expiry date ____ /____

To order: Mail or fax – photocopy or complete the order form above, and send your credit card details or cheque payable to: Australian Consolidated Press (UK), 10 Scirocco Close, Moulton Park Office Village, Northampton NN3 6AP, phone (+44) (01) 604 642200, fax (+44) (01) 604 642300, e-mail books@acpuk.com or order online at www.acpuk.com
Non-UK residents: We accept the credit cards listed on the coupon, or cheques, drafts or International Money Orders payable in sterling and drawn on a UK bank. Credit card charges are at the exchange rate current at the time of payment.
All pricing current at time of going to press and subject to change/availability.
Postage and packing UK: Add £1.00 per order plus 75p per book.
Postage and packing overseas: Add £2.00 per order plus £1.50 per book. **Offer ends 31.12.2008**